SURFING LEGENDS ALPHABET

Words by Robin Feiner

A is for Lisa **A**ndersen. Nicknamed 'Trouble,' this renegade ran away from home at 16, turned pro after one year and went on to win four world titles as a single mom. No wonder she was named as one of the 100 Greatest Sportswomen of the Century by Sports Illustrated for Women. Legend!

B is for Layne **B**eachley. With 'beach' in her name and surfing in her blood, this Aussie legend won six world titles in a row and seven overall. A renowned big wave surfer, she took on the men at Newcastle's 2004 EnergyAustralia Open, and battled a giant wave of depression as well.

C is for Corky Carroll.
This legendary goofy-footer from California's 'Golden Age' is considered to be the first professional surfer. Famous for his 'noseriding' and for charging in big surf, he won the U.S. Surfing Championship five times. In 1968, Corky was voted the No. 1 surfer by his surfing peers.

Dd

D is for Shane **D**orian. Equally comfortable in six and 60-foot waves, this gutsy Hawaiian, known simply as Dorian, has excelled as an ASP competitor, tow-in surfer and paddle-in specialist. In 2011, he won WSL's Ride of the Year, paddling into a 57-foot monster at Jaws.

E is for **E**ddie Aikau. Waimea Bay's first lifeguard, Eddie was legendary for saving over 500 lives and for charging giant waves. 'The Eddie' big wave contest is held in his honor whenever the surf is dangerously large – just like he loved it.

Ff

F is for Bernard Farrelly. 'Midget' became a giant star when he won the first World Surfing Championship in 1964 in front of 60,000 fans. Always a stylish surfer, he attributed his elegant lines to learning ballet with his sister as a child.

Gg

G is for Stephanie Gilmore. This guitar-loving Aussie earnt herself the nickname 'Happy Gilmore.' And with numerous world championships (including four consecutive wins), multiple CT victories and a prestigious 2010 Laureus World Sports Award to her name, it's pretty easy to see why.

H is for Bethany **H**amilton. In 2003, 13-year-old 'B-Ham' nearly died when a tiger shark took her left arm. But incredibly, she was back on her board and competing as a top pro within a month! Her inspirational story was shared with the world in the 2011 movie, 'Soul Surfer.'

I is for Andy **I**rons.
This iconic Hawaiian's fierce rivalry with Kelly Slater and unquenchable thirst for victory saw him become the people's champ. Winner of three world titles and four triple crowns, 'AI' is commemorated in Hawaii with Andy Irons Day on February 13.

Jj

J is for **J**ohn John Florence. Known as one of the dominant pipe surfers of his generation, 'JJ' is a master of hollow tubes, huge carves and gigantic airs. A two-time world champ and winner of 'The Eddie,' his laidback style influences millions.

Kk

K is for Duke **K**ahanamoku. The 'father of modern surfing,' Duke was a Hawaiian 'waterman' and Olympic swim champ famous for spreading surfing around the world. His demonstrations on giant redwood boards in California, Australia and New Zealand inspired thousands of people to take up surfing.

L is for **L**aird Hamilton. Known simply as 'Waterman,' this fearless big wave charger heads out when everyone else is heading in. And when he's not tackling 60-foot monsters, he's busy innovating crossover sports like tow-in surfing, stand-up paddleboarding and hydrofoil boarding.

M is for **M**ick Fanning. Nicknamed 'White Lightning' for his speed, Mick is a three-time world champ and winner of 22 Championship Tour events. An inspirational figure, he overcame the loss of his brother, a horrific injury and a punch-up with a Great White Shark to become an absolute legend.

N is for Greg **N**oll.
A legendary big wave charger from California, 'Da Bull' entered surfing lore on December 4, 1969, when he paddled into a giant wave at Mākaha. The 35-foot monster nearly destroyed him and, for the next 20 years, was known as 'the biggest wave ever ridden.'

**O is for Margo Oberg.
This trailblazer began to
beat the boys in local contests
at age 12. She won her first
world championship at 15
and became the world's first
pro female surfer in 1975.
Oberg went on to win seven
world titles and pave the
way for today's professional
female surfers.**

P is for Joel **P**arkinson. Regarded as one of the most stylish and gifted surfers of all time, 'Parko' was often underscored because he made the difficult look so easy. But in 2012, his effortlessly linked turns and silky-smooth maneuvers finally won this legendary Aussie a much-deserved world championship.

Q is for 'Queen of Mākaha,' Rell Sunn. An all-round water-woman, Rell was Hawaii's first female lifeguard and the No. 1 ranked amateur female surfer. Fearless and graceful in big waves, this inspirational legend co-founded the Women's International Surfing Association in 1975.

R is for Mark **R**ichards. Nicknamed 'Wounded Gull' for his outstretched arms and swooping turns, this Aussie champ was the greatest surfer of his generation. A four-time world champ between 1979 and '82, Richards was famous for his futuristic, progressive surfing and the legendary Superman logo on his boards.

S is for Kelly **Sl**ater.
This freakishly flexible Floridian has almost three times as many world titles as his nearest competitor. He is also both the youngest and oldest world champ, and is a winner of The Eddie Big Wave Invitational! No wonder this legend is known as 'King Kelly,' or simply The G.O.A.T.

T is for Tom Curren. Soul-surfer, style-master and progressive surfing pioneer, Curren is an inspiration to surfers everywhere. Renowned for his immaculate timing, fluidity and control, this natural-footed Californian acquired three world championships, 33 CT wins and a legendary status to rival Kelly Slater's.

U is for David Nuuhiwa. Arguably the greatest noserider ever, this smooth goofy-footer was widely regarded as the best surfer of the '60s, on both long and shortboards. With his unique flowing style, he won two United States Surfing Championship victories and was runner-up in the 1972 World Surfing Championship.

V is for **V**incent Sennen Garcia. Ironically nicknamed 'Sunny,' this Hawaiian tore waves apart with aggressive frontside hacks and vicious cutbacks. His power surfing and killer instinct won him six Triple Crowns, the 2000 World Championship and a reputation as a legendary 'hardman.'

Ww

W is for Wendy Botha.
Wendy's first world
championship was as a South
African in 1987, but her next
three ('89, '91, '92) came as a
naturalized Australian citizen.
Her success and dedication
quickly saw her become the
face of women's surfing.
She also worked tirelessly
to promote gender equality.

X is for **XX**L wave surfer Maya Gabeira. In 2013, Maya nearly drowned at Nazaré in a horrific big-wave wipeout. She bravely returned in 2018 to ride a 68-foot monster that went down in history as the largest wave ever surfed by a female. Hail to the Superwoman of surfing!

Y is for Nat Young.
At a time when surfing was all about 'flow,' Nat's aggressive high-speed approach and sharp turns earned him the nickname 'The Animal.' A world champ in 1966 and 1970, and winner of three Australian titles, Nat later wrote books on surfing, including one on 'surf rage.'

Z is for Frieda **Z**amba. Even though she disliked the limelight, this four-time world champ still managed to win five consecutive Surfer Magazine polls from 1985-1989. Lethal in small-to-medium surf and a master of power and progression, she is considered by many to be the greatest female surfer ever.

The ever-expanding legendary library

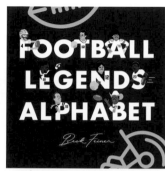

EXPLORE THESE LEGENDARY ALPHABETS & MORE AT WWW.ALPHABETLEGENDS.COM

SURFING LEGENDS ALPHABET
www.alphabetlegends.com

Published by Alphabet Legends Pty Ltd in 2020
Created by Beck Feiner
Copyright © Alphabet Legends Pty Ltd 2020

UNICEF AUSTRALIA
A portion of the Net Proceeds from the sale of this book
are donated to UNICEF.

978-0-6486724-5-6